Wh

written by Deborah Williams
designed by Laura McAlpin
illustrated by Gloria Gedeon

KAEDEN BOOKS™

I have a big head.

I have a little tail.

I have a short neck.

I have a long trunk.

I have ears shaped like fans.

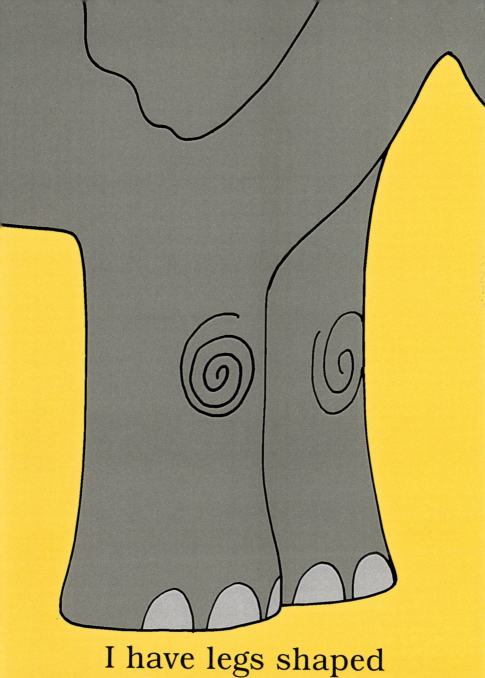

I have legs shaped
like tree trunks.

You can see me at the zoo.

You can see me at the circus.

I am an elephant.